POOLE
THEN & NOW

IN COLOUR

Ian Andrews & Frank Henson

The History Press

First published in 2012

The History Press
The Mill, Brimscombe Port
Stroud, Gloucestershire, GL5 2QG
www.thehistorypress.co.uk

British Library Cataloguing in Publication Data.
A catalogue record for this book is available from the British Library.

ISBN 978 0 7524 7965 1

Typesetting and origination by The History Press
Printed in India.

CONTENTS

ACKNOWLEDGEMENTS

The authors have derived material in this book from their own collections and acknowledge the help and permission they have received from many good friends who are the owners of often cherished family pictures, information and memories: M. Barber; M. Bailey; Birchmere Ltd; P. Broad; P. Clapcott; B. Dominey; G. Frend; B.J. Galpin; R. Gosling; D. Griffiths; Hall and Woodhouse Ltd; J. Hart; A. Hawkes; M. Hopkins; P. Horner; the late A.H. Moorman; I. Morris; M. Phillipson; Poole Historical Trust; Poole Museum and Local History Centre; F. Smith; Snaps (J. Roberts); M. Tombs; J. Waters; R. Welsh; P. Wilnecker; A. Yeatman; and K. Young.

Every effort has been made to obtain permission from copyright owners, and the authors apologise if any have been omitted or overlooked.

ABOUT THE AUTHORS

Passionate about Poole and its history, Ian Andrews was Town Clerk and Chief Executive Officer of Poole Borough Council from 1973, as well as Honorary Borough Archivist. He was a founder of Poole Heritage Forum, Wessex Newfoundland Society and several other local community organisations. Since retirement he has been elected President of the Society of Poole Men.

Formerly a Borough Councillor, Frank Henson is a lifelong resident of Poole. He is a member of the Wessex Newfoundland Society and the Society of Poole Men and frequently gives illustrated talks on the history of the area.

INTRODUCTION

'Ah... Poole. That's Sunseeker and Sandbanks, Lush and the Lifeboat HQ, isn't it? A beautiful place!'

The modern glimpses of Poole in this book disguise a long history of cross-Channel trade. Romans invaded Poole and valued the local clay and potteries. They established a legionary military fort in the area, linking to strategic roads. Liberation from manorial control was bought from the Lord of Manor who wished to raise money to go on the Fifth Crusade, evidenced in the town's first Charter dating from 1248.

Harbour trade came into its own as vessels grew larger and the shallow draught of the Saxon town of Wareham was insufficient. Poole was never a naval port, yet its ships and men fought for the King, while also pursuing the wool and pilgrim trades and exporting local beer. The town received rights of admiralty jurisdiction equal to the Cinque Ports in 1364. In 1405 they repelled an invasion by Spanish raiders as a reprisal for attacks by Harry Paye, a notorious Poole pirate.

It was an important yet never rich chartered market town (Leland described it in 1538 as recently 'much increased with fair building and use of merchandise... but... of old time a poor fishar village... covered in sedge and rushes'). In 1568 Queen Elizabeth I elevated it as a county in its own right, separate from Dorset and with its own sheriff and courts. At that time its pioneering sailors were braving the Atlantic, and by the eighteenth century played the leading UK role in the Newfoundland cod trade. Some of the remaining fine buildings reflect the wealth accumulated by the merchants of the day.

The town centre and quay were the centre of its economy, and housed many working people in squalid conditions. Photographs provide evidence of this, and this book contains examples where the old and the new photographs show alarmingly different scenes. Early in the nineteenth century, the boundaries of the town were enlarged and suburbs came into existence. It took until the twentieth century (and further extensions) for Poole's beaches and its tourist potential to become a reality. After an important war role, with D-Day and BOAC's flying boats providing the UK's only international airport for seven years, the town found its structure veering towards the elderly, traditional engineering industries declining and school leavers not getting jobs their good education deserved in their native town. Office jobs were limited and pay was low, especially for women. A bold and very successful programme of slum clearance, central redevelopment and industrial and residential expansion was undertaken by the council to counteract these problems.

The harbour remains a keystone in Poole's development and is again to the forefront as the elegant, bespoke Twin Sails bridge opens has been opened. Brownfield waterside sites will undergo regeneration as a result. To understand the future one needs to know and understand the town's past – its strengths and weaknesses. This book records a disappeared past and the new face and emphasis of a 'go-ahead' town.

POTTER'S ARMS

THIS PUB, AS its name implies, derives from the presence of nearby potteries and was rebuilt in its present form in 1927. The Patent Architectural Pottery on the opposite side of the road was established in the mid 1850s. Floor and wall tiles from this pottery adorn several buildings, notably the Poole Arms on Poole Quay. Working clay is thirsty work and the public house originally only sold beer, not gaining a full licence until 1955, when a skittle alley was added. The Royal and Ancient Order of Buffaloes' 'Pride of Hamworthy' Lodge No. 6278 met regularly in the pub.

WITH THE DEMISE of the pottery, the future of the pub would have been in doubt, but the trade now derives from the wider community of large areas nearby, redeveloped for housing, mainly as flats. With completion of the new Twin Sails Bridge between Hamworthy and Poole, further regeneration of the 13-hectare area of the former Generating Station site and the Carter Tiles and Sydenham factory sites over the next ten or fifteen years is expected to add some 5,000 or more residents within walking distance of the pub, and its future prosperity therefore seems assured.

POOLE QUAY TO
HAMWORTHY BRIDGE

THE OLD VIEW of Hamworthy Bridge dates from 1932 and shows an Anglo American
Oil Company petrol tanker after leaving the company's wharf at West Quay. The channel
between the quay and Hamworthy was first bridged by a wooden construction in 1834, at

a cost of £9,600, by the Lord of the Manor of Canford and local Member of Parliament, W.F.S. Ponsonby. Ponsonby, a Liberal, promoted a private Parliamentary Bill to get permission to build the bridge, to the annoyance of the Conservative controlled council. A toll of 1*d* was charged to cross the bridge. It was replaced in 1885 by an iron swing bridge to allow larger ships access to the wharves at West Quay. The council bought the bridge in 1926 for £16,000 and promptly abolished the toll.

THE PRESENT LIFTING bridge was constructed by the Cleveland Bridge Co. (recently involved in the building of the new Wembley Stadium and the new Twin Sails Bridge in Poole) at a cost of £60,000 and opened in 1927, to the cheers of many thousand of residents who lined the quay to witness the event. At the end of the twentieth century the quayside approaching the bridge was developed, and the Poole Lifeboat Station, berths and headquarters for the harbour pilot launches were added.

YEATMAN'S VICTORIA MILL

THE VICTORIA MILL of W.H. Yeatman & Sons dates back to merchant mariner Thomas Young in the early 1800s. The mill went through several changes of ownership before William Yeatman leased the buildings in 1880. The present frontage was added to the original mill in 1881. W.H. Yeatman & Sons was founded at Wareham in 1867. Their move to Poole saw the expansion of the business, which was fully concentrated on the site after a fire destroyed another company mill at Canford in 1884. The company bought surrounding premises to enlarge their quay production facilities. In June 1942 a delayed-action firebomb

destroyed the milling equipment and most of the production was suspended until after the war, when the mill was refurbished with more modern machinery.

PRODUCTION OF ANIMAL feedstuffs ceased in October 1974 when the company could no longer compete with their larger rivals. The last product to be made was several tons of pet rabbit pellets. The milling equipment was either scrapped or sold to other firms. After remaining empty for several months the buildings were gradually converted to alternative uses. The mill now houses the La Lupa restaurant, a shop over two floors, one office, ten flats and, at the rear, a lean-to shed workshop.

JUNCTION OF HIGH STREET AND THE QUAY

THE KINGS ARMS dates from the seventeenth century;
the Oakleys warehouse beyond, with a sack being lifted
on the hoist to an upper floor from a horse-drawn
wagon, is now a pizza parlour, with offices and a
penthouse above. It is now known as Newfoundland
House (note the flag flying from the roof garden).
The latter is the home of a direct descendant of an
eighteenth-century merchant family, the Jolliffes,
possibly the last such still living in the town.

THE PUB HAS gone through a succession of new
names in the last thirty years and may be familiar
to readers as the Helmsman, the Slurping Toad, the
Water's Edge, Hector's House and the Inn on the
Quay. It is currently called The Spotted Cow. To the
left, where schooners once docked, the corner of a
viewing platform can be seen, enclosing a modern
sculpture called 'Sea Music', created by one of
Britain's best-known living sculptors, Sir Anthony
Caro. It was built to distract attention from a massive
Wessex Water pumping station lying beneath it,
necessary to cope with town-centre sewage and raised
to survive any rising levels of sea that climate change
might bring about.

13

POOLE MUSEUM

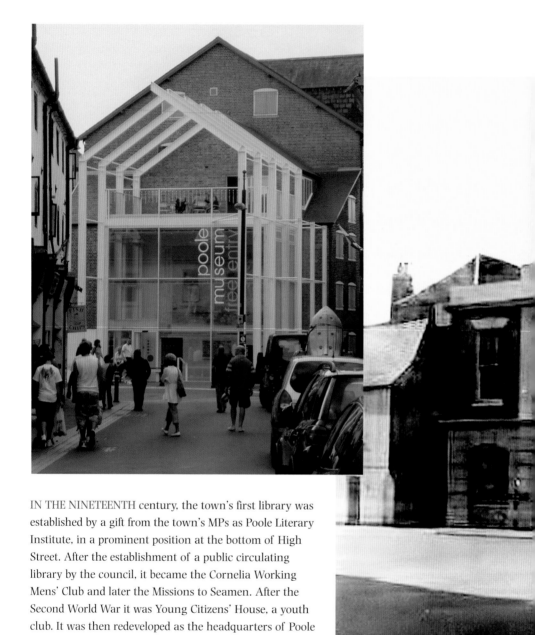

IN THE NINETEENTH century, the town's first library was established by a gift from the town's MPs as Poole Literary Institute, in a prominent position at the bottom of High Street. After the establishment of a public circulating library by the council, it became the Cornelia Working Mens' Club and later the Missions to Seamen. After the Second World War it was Young Citizens' House, a youth club. It was then redeveloped as the headquarters of Poole Harbour Commissioners, and when they moved out to the former Christopher Hill offices on the quay (later moving again to Hamworthy), it became the offices and entrance to the Maritime Museum and later the Waterfront Museum.

IN 2007 A major Lottery award enabled the council to completely remodel the building. It was renamed Poole Museum and the contents were rearranged to represent the whole of the town's history, with ever-changing displays and a shop, approached by a striking glass and steel entrance designed by the prizewinning international architect Richard Horden, a Poole native. The result is reflected in increased attendances. It includes a Local History Centre with many thousands of photos and other items accessible anywhere in the world on its website.

SCAPLEN'S COURT

IN 1923 STORMS blew down the chimneys and brick frontage of Scaplen's Court in High Street – which had been divided into at least eight tenements, with over thirty occupants, more than twenty years earlier – revealing a much older stone building, built in the 1400s. Its importance was soon recognized. The newly-formed Society of Poole Men stepped in to raise the money to purchase this Scheduled Ancient Monument, opening it as a museum, as the council displayed no interest until 1931, when it finally agreed to buy it. For many years it was open to the public under the name the Old Town House.

TODAY'S PHOTOGRAPH SHOWS Scaplen's Court Museum, roofed and restored to full height, in the original style, in 1986, with English Heritage's blessing. Nowadays the use of the museum is restricted to school parties, with the Society of Poole Men being allowed to hold one public open day a year. The garden at the rear of the house has been transformed in an attractive herb garden with access to it from the side, opened daily in the summer by an enthusiastic volunteer group.

BELBEN'S FLOUR MILL

BELBEN'S FLOUR MILL on the quay was one of many firms that dominated the waterfront and was an important employer in the town. The mill burnt down during the Second World War and the site was purchased by Christopher Hill Ltd for their head offices, with a weighbridge and product store attached. Christopher Hill's had several premises in the town and was a major manufacturer of animal feedstuffs. The company also exported several thousands tons of malting and animal-feeding quality barley every year. Christopher Hill Ltd was absorbed into the Ranks Hovis McDougall group in 1960 and later by Dalgety's. Poole Harbour Commissioners moved into the offices in the 1970s. The commissioners vacated the offices in the 1990s when they moved to the former clubhouse of Poole Yacht Club at Hamworthy.

WITH THE CHARACTER of the quay rapidly changing in the 1990s from a working dock to a leisure and tourist attraction area, which is important to the local economy, the offices became redundant and were pulled down. The present building incorporates a bar on the ground floor with flats above – some of which enjoy a balcony view of the quayside. The bar is extremely popular in the summer, as are all the many bars on the quay, when summer attractions include 'bikers' nights', on Tuesdays, fireworks and other family attractions on Thursdays and 'classic car' nights on Fridays, which bring thousands of visitors to the waterfront.

THE QUAY

FOR MANY GENERATIONS Poole Quay was a busy working dock with ships from other British ports and Europe bringing a variety of imports into the town as well as exporting local commodities such as clay for the British and Continental potteries. Until the introduction of motorised road transport, goods were carried by horse-drawn wagons and rail, with the rail track along the quay from the station at Nile Row continuing along West Quay Road. Also prominent in the background are the kilns of Carter, Stabler & Adams Pottery, who were the manufacturers of the world-famous fine Poole Pottery ware.

TODAY THE WATERFRONT has been transformed. The amusement arcade was formerly the last Newfoundland fish warehouse in Poole, but was later used by Christopher Hill Ltd to manufacture chicken and pig mash and meal. The Jolly Sailor and Lord Nelson Public Houses have survived, but sadly the pottery has succumbed to twenty-first

century pressures and, to the regret of the majority of local people, production was moved to Creekmoor and very quickly completely shut down. After demolition, the Pottery site was redeveloped with apartments and retail outlets in an architectural style sadly not reflecting local heritage or indigenous materials, and it is considered by many to be alien to the location. After much local pressure, a Poole Pottery plaque recording the part played by Poole at the D-Day landings – once on the old pottery wall – has been replaced on the new building.

EAST QUAY

THE OLD PICTURE shows East Quay, *c.*1930. The depth of water at the quay had become a problem in the 1890s as it was insufficient for larger ships to use the wharf. The quay was extended eastwards to obtain deeper water. This was important for the colliers delivering coal to the gasworks, as seen in the background of the picture. The coal was unloaded by the large overhead

grabs and transported very dustily to the main gas-making plant by overhead cableways across the lower town. When the gas-making plant was closed in 1968, the overhead gantries were dismantled.

TODAY A BOAT haven belonging to Poole Harbour Commissioners adjoins the quay, depriving the public of quayside car parking spaces with undisturbed views over the harbour. It caters for short-term and daily stays for visitors with vessels up to 35 metres. It has recently been awarded the top status of five Golden Anchors for service and quality.

THE SQUARE, HIGH STREET

W. J. BACON'S IRONMONGERS (later Bacon and Curtis Ltd) succeeded to a similar business established by G.S. Norton in an area of High Street that was known as the Square or Cornmarket. Used as a vegetable marketplace, it is now fenced off and used as forecourts under licence from the highway authority.

IN THE 1970s the Bacon and Curtis premises, which stocked every piece of ironmongery you could ever want, were demolished and redeveloped into offices known as Latimer House. They were first used by Barclays DCO Bank when it moved its headquarters to the town. The prominent buildings on the left are premises formerly occupied by a local bank, Poole Town and County Bank (which later became the Wilts and Dorset Bank), which grew rapidly in the eighteenth century as it was the bank used by the merchants in the then prospering Newfoundland trade. In turn this became the National Provincial Bank (now NatWest). During the Second World War the building was the Poole headquarters of the Royal Navy. With the reorganisation of the NatWest operations the bank was closed and, after a period of vacancy, the building is now used as Alcatraz Italian Restaurant.

HIGH STREET/ OLD ORCHARD

OLD ORCHARD LIES between Lagland Street and High Street. On the corner was Albert Satelle's tobacconists, which had another shop at 119a High Street. The workshop advertised by H.J. Cole and Sons, house furnishers and undertakers, was in Kendall's Alley, which ran from Lagland Street to High Street. The single-storey brick building on the left of the old picture was a rather smelly public toilet! A public car park was at the rear of the toilets and was replaced by a multi-storey block now called the Quay Visitors' Car Park. The road was widened in the early 1970s when the traffic flow of the lower town and High Street was re-routed.

IN THE BACKGROUND of the modern view are some of the flats that were built when the houses in the east of the Old Town were demolished. Behind hoardings on the right, a former Inland Revenue office has been converted to apartments with a Sainsbury's local supermarket at ground-floor level. The route (behind the viewer) from this location through Old Orchard leads directly to the new Twin Sails Bridge into town from Hamworthy in the west and the Holes Bay Road northerly to Fleetsbridge.

HIGH STREET

UNTIL THE DEVELOPMENT of the Arndale (Dolphin) Centre, the High Street was the hub of everyday shopping around the Old Town. Local retailers, many independent shop owners, catered for nearly all their customers' daily needs. This postcard of about 1930 shows prominently Midland Bank on the junction with Hill Street, then a modern building. The canopy on the left was in front of the entrance to the Amity Cinema. The Amity was originally a meeting hall. As a cinema it was popular with the children of the area with Saturday morning films. It also had a sweet kiosk in the entrance. In 1955 it was the scene of unruly incidents with the local 'Teddy Boys' when the film *The Blackboard Jungle* was shown, featuring Bill Haley and the Comets singing 'Rock Around The Clock'. Although only bicycles can be seen in the picture, and pedestrians strolling along the road, the High Street was a two-way thoroughfare and a bus route.

THE MODERN HIGH Street is now pedestrianised and tree planted, with seating for shoppers to rest. Family businesses, such as W.E. Boone's ironmongers, have nearly all gone. Many have been replaced by national chain stores, and a variety of charity shops. Amity Cinema closed in 1959. After demolition, a F.W. Woolworths store was built, but, with the closing of this chain, the shop is now a 'This Is It' retail shop. The Midland Bank is now part of the HSBC group and has relocated to 165 High Street, leaving the old building unoccupied. The High Street from the junction with Old and New Orchard northwards has been landscaped, and a street market is held on Thursdays as an added attraction.

URC CHURCH,
SKINNER STREET

SKINNER STREET CONGREGATIONAL church was built in 1777. The old chapel on the site, built in 1760 at a cost of £374 7s 7d, became an institute and later a school. It dominated the lower part of Lagland Street. Skinner Street Sunday School was the first in the town – the

earliest known reference to it was in 1787. The building was used as the British School on weekdays. The education was basic and children had to pay a fee of between a penny and tuppence a week. The original building had to be enlarged in 1833. Despite struggling at times, it continued as a school until the opening of South Road School in 1912.

THE LARGE HALL of the building was modernised and continues to be used by various organisations, but the school frontage was demolished in the 1980s. The railed-off area has opened up fine views of the listed Skinner Street (UR) church building. The next door New London Inn has been renamed The Cockleshell in honour of the small boat-raiding unit based at Hamworthy during the Second World War, whose exploits were immortalised in the 1955 film *The Cockleshell Heroes*, starring Trevor Howard, Anthony Newley, David Lodge and José Ferrer, who was also the director.

WEST QUAY ROAD (BDH)

IN 1940-41 BRITISH Power Boat Company, whose motto was 'Tradition, Enterprise, Craftsmanship', built a yard in West Quay Road in double quick time, to assemble wooden laminated Motor Torpedo Boats to the design of Hubert Scott-Paine. This work was so important to the war effort that bad weather was no deterrent and thirty boats were completed and launched before the factory was completed. When the war ended, the company used the skill of the staff to make prefabricated wooden housing to help relieve the housing shortage. This was a short-lived project and the buildings were bought by British Drug Houses and converted to chemical production, and this was a major employer in the borough.

IN 1987, AFTER a huge explosion at the storage depot opposite the main production facilities (occasioning the largest evacuation in the UK during peacetime), concern was expressed about the safety of the plant. Despite safety improvements on the site by BDH (a company that had latterly pioneered liquid crystal displays), a decision was made by subsequent owners, Merck Ltd, to end production at Poole by the end of 1998. After clearance, the site was purchased by the RNLI (whose national headquarters are in West Quay Road) for the erection of their college and training school. Designed by architects Poynton, Bradbury, Wynter Cole, the college was officially opened by the Queen in 2004. Lifeboat personnel from many countries also come to Poole to use the training facilities, now recognised as the finest in the world. A store building was made possible by a multi-million pound legacy from local businessman Bill Knott and is named after him.

HUNGER HILL

JOHN J. NORTON came to Poole from Andover and established a timber-importing business in 1872. By 1878 he was Poole's largest importer of timber, with thirty-three shiploads that year. The company office and yard opposite, in Towngate Street, was later used by Aish Electrical Contractors. John Norton was a leading figure in the Temperance Movement. Because of his beliefs he refused to attend the opening of the public library given to the town by him because of the alcohol served at the celebration.

NORTON'S WERE EVENTUALLY taken over by another Poole timber merchant, J.T. Sydenhams, and although the yard was maintained under the Norton name it was

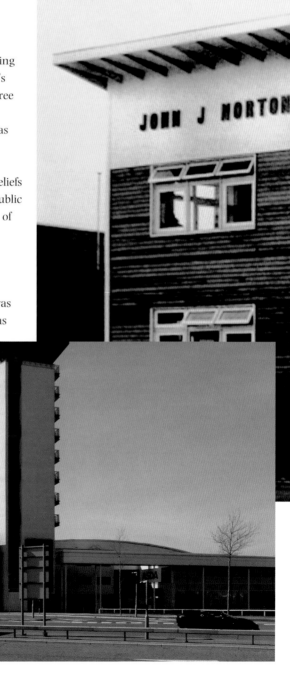

closed in the 1990s, by which time part of the yard had already been leased to Christopher Hill
Ltd and used as a store, paint shop and lorry garage. After the yard closed and Christopher Hill's
moved out, the large sheds were rented by an omnibus preservation society. After the sheds
were demolished, ASDA built a superstore with a block of residential flats adjoining the road.
During the building of the store, work was interrupted with the finding of phosphorus (a highly
inflammable material) that was left when part of the site was used as Balston's rope-work store
during the nineteenth and early twentieth centuries. This caused local traffic to be rerouted
until the site was made safe.

WEST QUAY ROAD

B. SHUTLER'S BOATYARD in West Quay
Road (pictured in around 1930) was on
the west shore, fronting Holes Bay. The
workmen in the picture are overhauling the
lifeboat *Harmar*, which served Poole between
1913 and 1938. Other work included speed
boats for Kay Don, a regular challenger
for the Harmsworth Speed Boat Trophy. In
1943, J. Bolson and Son Ltd took over the
premises and an adjoining timber yard, and
it played an important wartime role building
landing craft for the D-Day invasion.

AFTER THE WAR, the former Shutler
premises were sold to Christopher Hill Ltd
who installed a plant for the manufacture
of cattle and poultry foodstuffs. In 1961
they built a large grain-storage silo on
the site. After the closure of the animal
feeds mill, the site was derelict for several
years until ASDA opened a superstore on
part of it. Part of the remainder has been
developed as apartments. Plans for offices
and a hotel have been approved for the rest.

KINGLAND ROAD

AFTER THE DOLPHIN Centre (Arndale originally) was built, Kingland Road came to greater prominence as a bus terminus. These old cottages faced compulsory demolition, as there was to have been a new central police station on the site, only recently provided in Wimborne Road.

IN THE EVENT it was chosen in 1974 for the site of the Centre for the Arts, which was opened by HM the Queen in 1978. To keep it within the budget of accrued capital from the sale of (*inter alia*) land at South Canford Heath, various cuts were made to the original plans. The centre was fortunate to later obtain an Arts Council Lottery grant that enabled restoration of these items – and more besides – and was renamed Lighthouse on reopening. Now established as a major regional facility, in its most recent results it reports a small surplus, having presented 253 productions, delivered 1,265 performances or screenings and sold 217,119 tickets in the year.

POOLE PARK

WITH ITS SHALLOW depth, Poole Park saltwater lake has always been safe, even for inexperienced boat users. Arthur Shutler, seen here with some friends, was the first boat proprietor in the early twentieth century. Hand-operated paddleboats were available for children, with sailing dinghies and other craft for older customers, though originally sailing was not permitted on Sundays! Former Longfleet schoolboy Geoff Tapper had the concession from 1975 until 2002 and at its peak he had over 100 boats – a number which had been reduced to 25 by the time he retired. In the background of the picture is the bandstand, which was popular for brass-band concerts in summer months. The large houses in Parkstone Road, the homes of local businessmen, dominate the skyline.

VISITORS TO THE park have been able to enjoy refreshment since Edwardian days. The newest restaurant, Seven's Boat-Shed (originally Mezza Luna, which opened in June 2007), can be seen on the shore of the lake. In recent summers, potentially poisonous black algae plagued the lake and curtailed the boating activities. To combat midges, the sluice gates at the 'Bunny' have been opened in the winter by the council; this should drain the lake so that frost can lie on the edges and kill their larvae. The water has been dosed with blue dye to minimize the effect of sunlight. Islands have been constructed from dredged silt and planted with reeds to try and filter the water and also to encourage bird life. In addition, floating straw bales are also being used temporarily to accelerate the process. Boating is booming again now that Rockley Park Sailing School operates the concession. Apart from public hire, they provide sailing tuition in all sorts of craft for schools and schoolchildren.

ANYONE FOR TENNIS?

IN THE EARLY days of the twentieth century – and in line with way of life then – sports, boating and formal recreation were not allowed on Sundays in the park: it was more of a fashionable parade ground for perambulating. But by the 1920s tennis was all the rage on the

courts, in Poole Park and elsewhere. Players drew public attention and were dressed rather cumbersomely, even wearing hats. Long trousers were the order of the day for men, and white blouses and long skirts and white stockings for women. Spectators were also in their Sunday best.

THE POPULARITY OF the sport has waxed and waned over the years, with much less of a dress code and more comfortable and informal dress now prevailing. However, it is noticeable that it is not until after the All England Wimbledon matches are screened on television that the courts currently come into their greatest demand! In the present day, of course, the tennis courts are fenced to prevent stray balls or powerful aces from modern rackets going into the surrounding park and causing danger on its roads.

BAITER

IN 1909 IT was possible to look out from Whitecliff Road over a fine panoramic view of Baiter and across the harbour to Branksea Island, as it was then called. Notable Baiter buildings included the nineteenth-century Isolation Hospital (now demolished) and the even older Powder House of 1776 (now a ruin). All ships entering the harbour were required to deposit any gunpowder they carried in this store before docking. This was to prevent possible catastrophic accidents on the

quay involving sailing ships berthed several deep should an explosion occur. An early example of sensible Health and Safety regulation? The postcard was sent with Christmas greetings at 1.15 p.m. on Christmas Eve, with no doubt by the sender that it would reach its destination by Christmas Day!

TODAY, AS YOU drive along Whitecliff Road, it is possible to gain brief glimpses of Baiter, which is now joined to Whitecliff (itself a former pre-war rubbish tip reclaimed as an open space), after its reclamation and enlargement with pulverised rubbish. For many, this route through Poole Park is a bonus as they drive to and from the shops and offices in the Old Town.

COMMERCIAL ROAD

COMMERCIAL ROAD LEADS from the Civic Centre to the shopping centre at Parkstone. The Lloyds Bank branch was built in 1932 to meet the need for a 'resident banker' conveniently close to the brand-new Municipal Buildings. The adjoining petrol station (latterly a car showroom) was also a convenience until the 1960s, when safety legislation prevented the

service of fuel from swing pumps over the highway. And what would complete the needs of a new office? Well, a public house, of course, but fortunately one already existed in The Sloop, built in the 1820s before the railway arrived in Poole and when the sea came up to the original shoreline in what is now Poole Park. It was reportedly named after the wrecks of old sloops to be found on that shore.

WITH CHANGING TIMES signalling less use of cash in financial transactions, the bank was closed and has become a car dealership, also absorbing the forecourt of the petrol station. The Sloop has survived changes of name by the brewery. It was changed to The Conjurer's Half Crown, before that was shortened to the Conjurer and finally back to The Sloop. As the road markings show, this section of Commercial Road is now one-way, part of the Civic Centre road gyratory section.

ASHLEY CROSS

IN 1899 AN area Municipal Office was opened at the junction of Britannia and Salterns Road to serve the rapidly growing population of Lower Parkstone. Most of the housing in the area had coal-fired open hearths and chimney fires were a constant hazard. A fire engine took a long time to arrive from Poole. Thus the new offices also contained a long awaited horse-drawn fire appliance, with stables, to minimise the time taken to attend to a conflagration. Apart from the offices, there was a committee room also used as a reading room, which became Parkstone Library in 1927. On the right of the old picture is T. Moorshead's, a florist, fruiterer and greengrocer established in 1888.

POOLE FLYING BOAT Trust, remembering the years when Poole Harbour, with its flying boats, was Britain's only international airport linking with the Commonwealth, now uses the upper room in the library, for visitors and its archive. A Southern Electricity showrooms and offices replaced Moorshead's. Taylor's, a family butcher that later became a fish and chip shop, was demolished and is now incorporated in the highway verge. Southern Electricity's premises are now the print works of Minuteman. The former Central Hotel has been extensively refurbished and is now The Ox, with a fire pit where whole pigs and lambs are roasted in front of diners. The Ox has to compete with several other quality restaurants in the vicinity.

PARKSTONE GREEN

PARKSTONE GREEN, AS Parkstone Park is now known, was laid out by the council, in an area once known as Three Acres Field, in the late 1880s, at the same time as Poole Park, at a cost of £560 (including an elegant fountain). Providing a new park was one of Canon Ernest Dugmore's (then vicar of St Peter's church) campaigns for more recognition and better facilities for Lower Parkstone. It has been used freely for the Church's annual fête for many

years. It was a popular spot for nannies, pushing prams containing their charges, to meet up for conversation and, no doubt, to gossip about their employers!

IN 2011 THE park was renamed and extensively refurbished, with play equipment, a performance area, and a replacement for a hideous 1960s concrete fountain that had somehow replaced the original. Two new petanque courts are operated from the nearby Le Bateau restaurant. Events organised by the local businesses often draw large crowds, and Health and Safety regulations require that the area be temporarily fenced off. As it is not legal to charge for public access to the park, donations are sought by the organisers to cover the considerable cost of the fencing.

SALTERNS

THE SALTERNS, DERIVING from medieval salt recovery on the site, were surrounded by agricultural land, as seen by the grazing cows in the old photograph. The area became developed, along with the nearby Elms Estate, from the 1920s onwards. Desirable waterside

properties, some in art deco style, enjoyed extensive harbour views and were near to yachting facilities if they lacked their own private jetty.

IT COULD HAVE been very different: at the end of the First World War, a desperate need for merchant shipping to replace wartime losses gave rise to a plan – supported by both Poole Council and the Harbour Commissioners, in conditions of great secrecy – to transform a nearby area and a pier that had served for the export of pottery products, and there to establish a major shipyard. However, the government, whose support was required, stepped in and directed that such development should instead be based on the Clyde!

SALTERNS BOATYARD

BOAT BUILDING HAS been a local craft in Poole Harbour ever since the earliest settlements in the area. This was endorsed by the discovery of an Iron-Age log canoe craft by local fishermen off Brownsea Island in 1964. This ancient boat is a prized exhibit in Poole Museum. With

the expansion of the Newfoundland trade, local merchants had many of their boats built by local tradesmen at yards located around the quay and Lower Hamworthy. As the popularity of yachting and yacht racing increased in the later nineteenth century, smaller yards were established. Walton Yacht and Launch Works, Lilliput, was one of four local boat builders listed in Poole in 1936. The yard was approached by an inlet next to the Harbour Club at Salterns, built by the landlady of the Sea View Hotel for her son's employment.

THE MODERN PICTURE shows the construction of new workshop facilities and the building of larger residential houses on the shoreline as the area has increased in popularity over the last seventy years. Pizey's Pier, which can be seen in the background of the old photograph, has been demolished, but many of the newer properties have built their own landing stages.

FLAG FARM

FLAG FARM, IN the distance, was a remote farm from at least Tudor times, approached by dusty tracks bordering the harbour, and was a landmark from both land and sea. It is said to have links with Isaac Gulliver, a notorious smuggler who reputedly reformed his ways when he married a

local banker's daughter. Sewage used to be conducted out to sea through cast-iron pipes until the council was the first in the area to reverse the flow and take the town's sewage to an inland treatment works. A seawall constructed over the sewer survives today, surmounted by splendid dolphin lamp posts. Shore Road was not metalled until the 1930s and a beach visit involved a dusty trek.

ON A BREEZY day, the shallow Whitley Lake is a popular spot for wind and kite surfing and is still well used for gathering shellfish and bait at low tide. When the prevailing gales blow from the south west, this stretch of road can flood from the spray over the wall and the stream flowing from Parkstone Golf Course through Luscombe Valley (now a local nature reserve).

SANDBANKS

IN THE 1890S, concern that the sea might break through Sandbanks if a training bank and deeper entrance to the harbour was created without protective groynes led to lengthy acrimony with the owner of the peninsula, Lord Wimborne, over who should pay the cost. In 1892, he even offered almost the whole of Sandbanks' peninsula (except the foreshore) to the council for free in return for erecting groynes and works to prevent the sea breaking through it. The area was barren sand, desolate and used mainly by weekend fishing and wildfowl shooting parties. Local legend says that building sites were then offered by Lord Wimborne (actually leased with an option to purchase later) for as little as £10 an acre, and many locals built bungalows – or

even sheds, shacks or railway carriages – for summer holiday getaways. Very few main homes were built. Sandy Hollow (in the old picture) was a sandy track in this sparsely developed area in the 1920s, near to the landmark of the crest of High Horse Manger, the highest point on the peninsula.

THE SUCCESS OF THE SCHEME, coupled with a desire to live in an attractive area close to the magnificent sea views, has led to an enormous rise in land values at Sandbanks. It is now the fifth most expensive area in the world, after certain parts of London, Tokyo, New York and Hong Kong. In 2012, Lord Wimborne's Canford Estate decided to sell off even the retained foreshores with a guide price of £50,000 to £100,000 each. Sandy Hollow has been renamed Grasmere Road, and all the old buildings have disappeared. Because of the type of detached housing it has been able to retain a more open atmosphere than many of the apartment blocks on nearby Banks Road as it approaches the Sandbanks-Studland ferry. Today, when the trees are in full foliage, the view to High Horse Manger is sadly obliterated.

SANDBANKS BEACH

IN POST-WAR days, early morning bathers and dog walkers at Sandbanks would have encountered the unusual sight of racehorses training on the beach! Mrs Louie Dingwall, the first female trainer to be recognized by the Jockey Club, had her stables in Panorama Road nearby. The horses she trained included one named Poole Park, owned by Freddy Rowe, a wealthy local builder and former mayor and alderman of the borough. Before she married, Miss Foott, as she then was, owned, ran and used to drive buses on a route still known today as the Rossmore Flyer, serving Upper Parkstone's side roads.

SINCE 2008, HORSES have once again commanded attention on the beach for a prestigious world beach polo event, attracting many free-spending socialites to the resort. The public are allowed a free view from a bespoke sandbank on the seaward side. For 2012 the event included a race between a horse and a sports car. The former won! This beach has proudly earned a Blue Flag for its facilities ever since the awards began.

CANFORD CLIFFS PARADE

BOTH BRANKSOME ESTATE to the east and Canford Cliffs to the west were heath and forest
land running along the top of the cliffs bordering Poole Bay, familiar in old days only to the local
smugglers and Preventive (Customs) men. Sales of the estate land commenced in the 1880s, and

many fine marine residences, some with accommodation for live-in staff, date from those early days. When the Canford Cliffs Estate was developed in the late nineteenth century and early twentieth century, its shops in The Parade were suited to meet the needs of the maids, servants and cooks who sought everyday goods for the 'charmingly situated' marine houses they served. A chemist, grocer, fishmonger, dairy, butcher and baker were essential, together with a greengrocer, drapers, decorator and ironmongers.

WITH THE DECLINE of domestic servants and the increase in motor-car ownership, many residents went further afield to larger shops with more choice to purchase their requirements. The local outlets began to fail. After their closure, coffee shops and restaurants moved in, creating a Continental atmosphere. Banks and estate agents, which seem twenty-first century necessities, have also moved into the Parade. Only the motor trade seems to endure, but – since the abolition of over-the-pavement swing-arm petrol pumps – only as a repair garage and showroom. A post office and a telephone exchange also survive.

BRANKSOME CHINE,
LOOKING WEST

FOR CENTURIES THE isolated cove of Branksome Chine was the ideal location for smugglers to land their contraband away from the eyes of the local Preventive Officers. The natural landscape offered many secret hiding places where, after landing, the goods could be collected at leisure. By the early twentieth century the main visitors to the Chine were local fishermen. They could

leave their boats on the sand without fear of theft or vandalism. The horse in the background was the only means of transport and may have been used to haul the boats out of the sea. In the 1930s workers started to be granted more holidays by their employers and wanted to get away from home for a rest. In the 1930s Poole started to realise the importance of tourism – despite opposition from some councillors – and the beaches were a natural attraction to holidaymakers.

TO CATER FOR the needs of holidaymakers, an art-deco solarium – now the upmarket Branksome Beach Restaurant – was built to boost the sun's rays. To arrest the erosion of the crumbling cliffs, tons of sand were removed and used as infill at Branksome Recreation Ground in Alder Road, as an unemployment relief scheme in the 1930s. A concreted promenade was also built, with wooden beach huts available for renting. These were replaced by concrete structures in the 1960s. To shorten the waiting list, at the time of writing, the council are consulting on a proposal that would limit rental of all the huts for five or ten years maximum, sparking opposition from long-term tenants, many of whom had waited ten years or more to get their huts and who say there are a number of sites where additional huts could still be built.

BRANKSOME CHINE,
LOOKING EAST

THE VISITOR AMENITIES at Branksome Chine were, at first, very basic. The adjacent small marquee served as a café. Over the next twenty years these facilities were extended to a hotchpotch of other small huts, with a small car park for a few cars. The café charged visitors for hot water to brew their own tea on the beach, 1d for a small teapot, 2d for a larger one. An old oil drum was used as a litterbin. Two bicycles, the popular mode of transport, were left

unattended against one of the huts. In 1927 the proprietors of the attractions were a Mr Strange and Harry and Emma Fletcher.

IN 1930s THE council realised that popular holiday and tourist beaches needed more attractive modern facilities. The advance of ownership of motor vehicles and more regular public transport services brought an increase in the number of beach visitors. Clean public toilets, private changing cubicles and extended car park were provided. Except for a large increase in car parking fees, very little has changed since the 1930s development was built.

POOLE
ROAD

THE SHOWROOMS OF F. English Ltd, Poole Road, Branksome, built in 1958, with a garage workshop and petrol filling facilities, broke the Branksome Park strict building conventions and was bitterly opposed by the local residents. F. English Ltd, owned by Col. Ronnie Hoare, was the local agent for Ford's and, when the company moved in the late 1980s to a newly built facility at Tower Park, the premises were used briefly as an indoor market, with a second hand car dealer on the outside car park.

TESCO PURCHASED THE site in the early 1990s and submitted plans for a supermarket – also unsuccessfully opposed by the local residents. After the opening of Tesco in 1993, the filling station continued for several years as an independent business until Tesco eventually took it over.

THE WOODMAN

THE WOODMAN PUBLIC House in Poole Road, Branksome, was built in around 1855 by the Durweston Brewery, which later amalgamated with Hall and Woodhouse. It was very popular as a convenient stopping-off place for travellers on the dusty road to Christchurch. When Bournemouth developed a short distance along the road in the late nineteenth century, it was

the nearest licensed premises to the town until the Westbourne Hotel was built. All the main line railways to and from London and Bath went to Poole, and the post for just-emerging Bournemouth was handled by the Poole postmaster – their post was handed over at a meeting in the pub!

IN 1968 THE original pub was closed, much to the disappointment of the regular clientele. Ten-pin bowling was the new fashionable indoor sport and permission was obtained to demolish the building and provide a bowling alley complex with a new Woodman alongside. Unfortunately the replacement pub has not been able to recreate the cosy atmosphere of the original building.

ASHLEY ROAD, BRANKSOME

IN 1912, ASHLEY Road, Branksome, was a busy suburb of Poole. Until 1905, it had been independent of the town as a separate urban district, evidenced by its offices in Library Road, now known as Bob Hann House. Bournemouth Council had been keen to annex the area, but was defeated. The tram service, driven by an overhead power supply suspended from ornate poles, ran between Poole, Upper Parkstone and County Gates. It started in 1901 and ran until Hants and Dorset Motor Services Ltd introduced a substitute bus service in June 1935. The original tram fare from Albert Road to County Gates was 1*d*, with 3*d* the fare to Poole railway station at Towngate Street.

THE CHARACTER OF this stretch of road has largely been retained, as many of the shops are still independent traders. Where any redevelopment has taken place it is usually in the form of flats. Efforts are currently being made to re-establish a Chamber of Trade to serve the area, seek improvements and ensure its decoration at Christmas and similar festivals as the council no longer undertake this. There is a popular modern library with free terminals and internet access.

RICHMOND ROAD/ ASHLEY ROAD JUNCTION

THESE PHOTOGRAPHS ILLUSTRATE the changes in Ashley Road, looking east from Richmond Road (formerly Sandy Lane junction) between 1945 and the present day. Poole and Parkstone Co-operative Society's department store on the left is now largely The Parkstone, a public house. The prominent white building beyond it was the Regal Cinema, which opened

as the Victoria Palace in 1921 and was modernised in 1937, closing in 1963. The final film was *Come Blow Your Horn*, starring Frank Sinatra. On its site a Boots chemist, a betting office and an Iceland store now trade. Further in the distance, Co-op retain a food supermarket built on the site of a former Butler's furnishing store.

SADLY, WOOLWORTHS HAS ceased trading and also a successor 99p store. Coopers' discount store has now started trading in this store. On the right, note how former tram poles have been converted into street lights and how a Belisha beacon then coped with pedestrians crossing, though without the zebra markings at that date. With increased numbers of cars, a traffic-light system with a pedestrian phase and safety barriers has been installed.

SEA VIEW ROAD/ RINGWOOD ROAD, NEWTOWN

AS THE NAME suggests, Ringwood Road was the main route from Poole to Ringwood. It was originally a turnpike road; a charge was levied on horse-drawn vehicles to use the road. The tollhouse was situated near the George Hotel. Until the early twentieth century it was an unmade surface going through Newtown. The most prominent building in the old picture is the post office in the middle of the road junction. Sea View Road (on the left of the picture) leads to Constitution Hill and a splendid viewpoint over the harbour. Telegraph poles can be clearly seen, but there were no streetlights. Who would dare stroll in the middle of the highway today without fear of being killed or injured?

TODAY, TRAFFIC LIGHTS are needed to regulate the traffic flows and this is one of the busiest road junctions in the borough. The building of housing and industrial estates in the area as well as through traffic has made for heavy use of Ringwood Road, especially during rush hours. The trees at the edge of Ringwood Road are among the few survivors of the grand plan by Borough Engineer Ernest Goodacre to distinguish all the main roads leading to Poole with such planting in the verges. Tree roots and road widening schemes have taken their toll on some of the trees.

LONGFLEET

THIS POST-WAR panorama of Longfleet shows Parkstone and Longfleet Roads converging. The twin chimneys of the Generating Station at Hamworthy, in the background, dominated views from miles around from 1948 until they were demolished in 1993. This part of Poole

arose as an overspill suburb of the crowded Old Town from about 1830 onwards and the streets are lined with Victorian villas. Many of these are now in commercial use or provide accommodation for staff from the nearby hospital.

THE LANDMARK BUILDING in the modern view housed the headquarters of the Dominion, Colonial and Overseas branch of Barclays Bank, relocated from the City of London. It processed all the bank's travellers' cheques and required modern electronic links. Such is the speed of change in technology that a further review of its function has led the Bank to require less staff and space, leaving part of the premises to be leased to new occupants. The symbolic eagle that dominated the building has now been dismantled. Both old and new shots were taken from the roof of the Nurses' Home.

POOLE HOSPITAL

LADY CORNELIA WIMBORNE, an aunt of Winston Churchill and a great benefactor to Poole, provided a hospital in West Street. When this proved to be too small, it transferred to The Hermitage in Weston's Lane and later still to Sir Peter Thompson's House in Market Street. Her offer to donate a cottage hospital to celebrate Queen Victoria's Golden Jubilee in 1887 was rejected in favour of a new library, donated by J.J. Norton, a local timber merchant and well-known leader of the teetotal movement. By 1906 it was obvious that larger facilities were required and Lord Wimborne gave 2.5 acres of land next to Longfleet church for a new hospital, named after his wife, Cornelia. The new hospital opened in 1907. During the First World War, soldiers injured fighting in Europe were brought by train to the already expanded hospital for treatment.

WITH NUMEROUS FURTHER expansions these buildings survived until 1962, when the hospital was completely redeveloped. Princess Alexandra laid the foundation stone for the new buildings, opening a new maternity unit, in St Mary's Road, the same day. By 1964 A Block, the first part of the hospital, was in use. Building, including a Nurses' Home, continued rapidly and the Queen opened the main part of the hospital in July 1969. Many units and much equipment has been added, some paid for by generous donations from local benefactors. Poole Hospital became a NHS Trust in 2007. In 2012 plans for the first merger of foundation trusts in the UK between Poole and the Royal Bournemouth and Christchurch Hospitals were revealed.

FERNSIDE ROAD

FERNSIDE GARAGE, OWNED by A.H. Moorman, was situated at No. 137 Ringwood Road. A greengrocer, fruiterer, wool shop, tobacconist and hairdresser occupied adjoining shops, with residential flats above. In the 1970s, after Mr Moorman retired, the block was rebuilt as a Total fuel station, with a small garage workshop attached.

WITH THE CLOSURE of the filling station, just one of many in the town that have closed since the advent of petrol stations attached to superstores, there was a further redevelopment of the site with a One-Stop convenience store, now one of the many Tesco Express outlets in Poole that always seem to be very busy, with cars queuing on the main road to occupy spaces in its tiny car park.

83

TOWN POUND

OPPOSITE THE TESCO Express in the previous photograph was the original Longfleet Pound, where stray farm animals were secured until collected by their owners. There were three other pounds in the town, at Hamworthy, Newtown and aptly named Pound Street in the Old Town. These pounds recall the days when the town had more farmland and husbandry was an important occupation. Pound Lane was still mainly a rough track that was very popular for blackberry pickers.

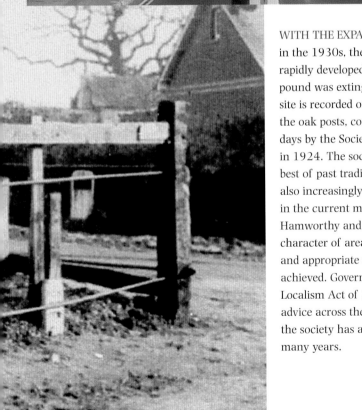

WITH THE EXPANSION of house building in the 1930s, the Longfleet farmland was rapidly developed and the need for the pound was extinguished. The history of the site is recorded on the sign hanging from the oak posts, commissioned in its early days by the Society of Poole Men, founded in 1924. The society seeks to preserve the best of past traditions and buildings, but is also increasingly involved in ensuring that, in the current massive redevelopment of Hamworthy and West Quay, the distinctive character of areas and buildings is respected, and appropriate use of local materials is achieved. Government legislation in the Localism Act of 2011 and revised planning advice across the UK give backing to the role the society has already played in Poole over many years.

BUSHELL MILL

AS THE NAME suggests, Bushell Mill Farm was
for centuries in the ownership of the Bushell
family. In 1910 the farm was purchased by George
and Percy Bailey, already farming at the nearby
Milestone Farm and Dairy that was opposite
the New Inn. The Bailey family also owned the
Creekmoor Mill. The dairy herd could be observed
grazing from Wimborne Road. Also attached to
the 36-acre farm was an abattoir, and senior
residents of the area can remember animals being
driven along Wimborne Road from Poole Railway
Station to the farm for slaughtering. The picture
shows George Bailey Snr outside Bushell Mill
farmhouse in the 1930s.

IN 1964, AFTER the death of George Bailey
Snr, Bushell Mill was sold to property developers
Comben and Wakelin for housing development.
Mr Comben was a Quaker and forbade any outlet

selling alcohol on the site, but that was rendered irrelevant as the Fleets Bridge Hotel is next to the estate. Before the purchasers could inspect the farm some bulrushes had to be cut down as they indicated an area of low-lying ground that flooded easily with the run-off from the peat-laden Canford Heath. When the roads were laid out references to the previous owners of the farm were kept in the names of Bushell Mill Road and Bailey Crescent.

NAG'S HEAD FARM, WATERLOO ROAD

NAG'S HEAD FARM, Waterloo Road, was a dairy (latterly known as Bennett's Dairy), but it was originally built in 1819 by Gibbs of Wimborne as a beerhouse with its own brewhouse. Then known as The Nag's Head Inn, it was one of the last licensed premises in the town on the road to Wimborne. The inn also provided stabling for travellers. The public house closed in 1883. The Bennett Family moved to Nag's Head in 1918 from Oakdale Road to expand their dairy herd and milk delivery business. The family were members of the Plymouth Brethren Church and built a chapel for their fellow worshippers on land near the farmhouse when an old chapel at

Old Orchard was demolished. Nag's Head Farmhouse was demolished in 1975 to enable the widening of Waterloo Road and the laying out of Cabot Lane. The northern part of the farmland had previously been sold for playing fields when Parkstone Grammar School relocated to Sopers Lane from Ashley Cross in the early 1960s.

A VARIETY OF businesses, including a motor servicing garage and tyre fitter and an eatery, now occupy the Waterloo Road frontage where once an impressive building stood. The Bethany Chapel, now owned by the school, is still in the school grounds and can be seen from Waterloo Road.

CREEKMOOR LANE

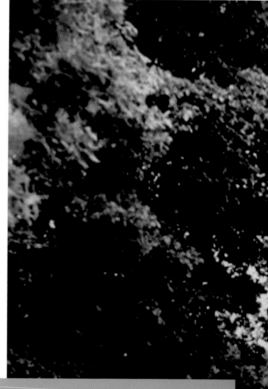

CREEKMOOR WAS A small backwater off Holes Bay with a closely knit small community. The area was extremely prone to regular flooding during very high tides, especially if accompanied with severe weather conditions. Creekmoor Lane was the main thoroughfare leading to two sandpits and brickworks, a few small farms, a post office, the local grocery stores and the village hall. Creekmoor also had a small railway halt, mainly to serve the employees of the Royal Ordinance Factory at nearby Sopers Lane. A white post marks the entrance to the old Creekmoor Mill House (now demolished).

THE INFILL OF the shoreline and new modern drainage technology opened up Creekmoor for development. With the pressure for more housing in Poole, the area was rapidly expanded in the 1970s with a mix of social and private residences. A supermarket, public house and church have been built to serve the area. The Millfield Estate is on the right of the picture; however, some of the old rural features remain, like the oak trees, which can be seen in the old picture and are still there today.

BROADSTONE STATION

'CASTLEMAN'S CORKSCREW' WAS the original main line to London from Dorchester via Brockenhurst and Southampton. To travel directly to London, Poole passengers had to join the train at Broadstone until Poole Station and the line via Bournemouth was opened in 1872. The Pines Express from Manchester to the resorts of Poole and Bournemouth also ran through Broadstone Station by way of the Somerset and Dorset Railway (nicknamed the 'Slow and Dirty') as far as Bath. The S & D railway served many rural villages, and was lost to passenger traffic in 1966 in the Beeching cuts. Its loss continues to be regretted. To the right in the old photograph, Lavender Farm can be seen.

BROADSTONE LEISURE CENTRE and the adjoining car park now occupy the site of the station and track. The local lavender industry, after which the farm was named, has now ceased. The nearby Broadstone Railway Hotel has recently reopened to customers as the 'Goods Yard'. Nowadays a footpath/cycleway runs from Poole town centre to the northern extremity of the borough along the route of part of the former rail track, known as 'Castleman's Trail'.

MOORTOWN

IN FORMER YEARS a typical and likely business to find in a remote rural part of northern Poole was the wheelwright and carriage- and wagon-building works of H.A. Gane, in what was then Kinson tithing. (This part of Kinson tithing, including Broadstone, Merley, Canford

and Ashington, was incorporated in the Borough of Poole in 1933.) A wide range of carts and carriages was made on the site and wind power was used to drive the belt-driven machinery, as mains electricity had not yet reached the area.

THE EXACT LOCATION is now hard to trace, but bears resemblance to the farm at Moortown pictured on a site that runs down to the River Stour.

If you enjoyed this book, you may also be interested in…

Haunted Poole

JULIE HARWOOD

From heart-stopping accounts of apparitions, manifestations and related supernatural phenomena to first-hand encounters with spirits, this collection of stories contains new and well-known spooky tales from in and around Poole, including legendary Poole pirate Harry Payne and his ghostly galleon, the screams of Alice Beard and spectral beggars wandering the streets. This incredible gathering of ghostly goings-on is bound to captivate anyone interested in the supernatural history of the area.

978 0 7524 4503 8

Dorset Folk Tales

TIM LAYCOCK

These lively and entertaining folk tales from one of Britain's most ancient counties are vividly retold by local storyteller Tim Laycock. Their origins lost in the oral tradition, these thirty stories from Dorset reflect the wisdom (and eccentricities) of the county and its people.

978 0 7524 6636 1

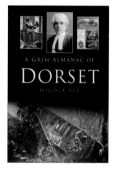

A Grim Almanac of Dorset

NICOLA SLY

A Grim Almanac of Dorset is a day-by-day catalogue of 365 ghastly tales from around the county. Full of dreadful deeds, strange disappearances and a multitude of mysteries, this almanac explores the darker side of the Dorset's past. Generously illustrated, this chronicle is an entertaining and readable record of Dorset's grim past. Read on … if you dare!

978 0 7524 5884 7

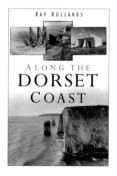

Along the Dorset Coast

RAY HOLLANDS

Ray Hollands has walked the entire Dorset coastline to capture its unique atmosphere through his eye-catching photography. The dramatic and constantly-changing nature of this part of Britain's coast is depicted here, as well as an eclectic mix of bays, harbours, cliffs and beaches, and the stunning countryside bordering the sea. From bustling resorts, like Bournemouth and Weymouth, to places of quiet solitude, all are shown to great effect here. This book is sure to capture the imagination of anyone who knows and loves the county.

978 0 7524 5185 5

Visit our website and discover thousands of other History Press books.

www.thehistorypress.co.uk